Original title:
Under the Canopy

Copyright © 2025 Creative Arts Management OÜ
All rights reserved.

Author: Olivia Sterling
ISBN HARDBACK: 978-1-80566-604-2
ISBN PAPERBACK: 978-1-80566-889-3

Veins of the Earth

In the soil, worms wiggle with glee,
They host dance parties for ants, you see.
Rocks hold secrets, grumpy and old,
While mushrooms giggle, their stories unfold.

Roots tie their shoes, they race for the light,
But trip on the shadows in a silly fight.
Laughter erupts from beneath leafy sheets,
As crickets play tunes and tap their small feet.

Lullabies of the Leafy Realm

In the shade where squirrels dance,
Frogs sing tunes, take a chance.
Breezes whisper silly jokes,
While the ants plan tiny hoaxes.

Beneath the branches, dreams take flight,
Listen close, but hold on tight.
Snails race on a dewy track,
Laughing as they bounce right back.

The sun peek-a-boos with a wink,
As creatures gather, laugh, and think.
A turtle tells tales of the past,
While butterflies twirl, oh what a blast!

In dappled light, the shadows play,
With crickets chirping a cabaret.
Each leaf a stage for jesters bold,
In this leafy realm, laughter unfolds.

Trails Through the Greenery

Squirrels debating who's the king,
They chatter and dance in a wild swing.
A rabbit slips, oh what a sight,
While hedgehogs gossip beneath the light.

A frog leapt high to catch some fame,
He missed a fly and found it lame.
Through bushes thick, a trail they roam,
Welcome to the forest, it's their home!

Twilight Beneath the Boughs

As darkness falls, a raccoon plots,
With a snack of berries, he ties up knots.
Owls hoot softly, they tell tall tales,
While fireflies glow, wearing their veils.

A turtle's slow, but thinks he's fast,
He sways in rhythm, a dance unsurpassed.
The stars poke through, and critters prance,
Twilight's here, let's take a chance!

Mysteries of the Grove

Mice in a meeting, plotting a heist,
For breadcrumbs dropped, oh that would be nice!
Roots whisper secrets of long-lost gnomes,
And snails debate how to build tiny homes.

A clever crow with a shiny prize,
Is chased by a jay, oh what a surprise!
In this tangled mess of trees and games,
Even the shadows have silly names!

Dance of the Leafy Veil

Leaves sway gently, looking quite dapper,
A beetle spins, oh what a caper!
Grasshoppers laugh with a playful leap,
As the sun dips down, they start to creep.

With a gust of wind comes the big show,
Flowers swaying, putting on a glow.
Underneath this playful array,
Nature's laughter brightens the day!

Timelessness in the Thicket

In the thicket, squirrels race,
Chasing shadows, what a chase!
Leaves gossip, rustle, speak,
Underfoot, the rabbits sneak.

Time stands still, a funny show,
Bumbling bears say, "Oh no!"
Though they trip on roots so wide,
Nature giggles, can't decide.

Cerulean Skies Through Green

Blue above, a silly sight,
The birds argue, who takes flight?
A parrot wears a bowler hat,
While worms play poker, fancy that!

Trees sway, dance with glee,
Twirling leaves, such jubilee!
A gust of wind, they start to spin,
Nature's party, let the fun begin!

Pathways of Light and Shadow

In light and shadow, snails parade,
With tiny hats, a grand charade.
They slide on trails, so smooth and slick,
While ants audition for a magic trick.

Fungi giggle, mushrooms sway,
Whispering jokes of yesterday.
A sunbeam whispers, "Join the fun!"
In this realm, we're never done!

Embracing the Green Overhead

Above, the leaves wiggle and weave,
Like green dancers, hard to believe.
A chameleon slips, colors change,
While frogs leap in a range so strange.

Laughter bubbles from the brook,
With fish that read the strangest book.
Each ripple sends a ticklish shout,
In this world, we laugh, no doubt!

Radiance in the Hollow

In a hollow so bright, where squirrels play,
They build tiny homes, in a cheeky way.
A raccoon with style, wearing a hat,
Dances around, oh look at the cat!

The sunlight beams, through leaves it glows,
A rabbit in shades, striking poses like pros.
With a wink and a hop, they hold a parade,
While a wise old owl rolls his eyes, dismayed.

Echoes Among the Spruce

Spruce trees whisper secrets, so slinky,
While birds gossip loudly, though a bit kinky.
A chipmunk jumps high, showing off moves,
While a sleepy snake just watches and snooze.

Twitching their tails, the critters all grin,
A dance-off begins, oh what a din!
The trees sway along, keeping perfect time,
As a squirrel throws acorns, declaring 'I'm prime!'

The Sanctuary of Twisting Vines

Vines intertwine, making a nest,
Where hedgehogs compete to find who's the best.
A juggling platypus steals the show,
While frogs leap and croak, shouting, 'Let's go!'

One beaver winks, crafting a den,
As a team of raccoons gather again.
With giggles and splashes, they create a scene,
In this park of mischief, it's silly but keen.

A Tapestry of Trees

Trees gather round, a quirky ball,
With branches all tangled, they're having a hall.
A moose in a tux, struts proudly and bold,
While a bear in a dress simply can't be controlled.

The cake on the grass, oh what a sight,
Made of sweet berries, all arranged just right.
But a raccoon sneaks up, with a nibble so sly,
Stealing the cherry! Oh, my oh my!

Fragments of Forest Lore

In the woods, where squirrels play,
They plot the nutty heist each day.
The rabbits giggle, tossing leaves,
As owls just shrug and roll their sleeves.

A deer told jokes to trees so tall,
But the trees just stood, not laughing at all.
The fox, meanwhile, danced in glee,
Said, 'Hey, who knew it'd be this zany?'

Harmony Beneath the Flora

The flowers had a real debate,
On who smelled best, it got quite great!
'You're so sweet, it makes me sick!'
Said one, and then they giggled quick.

The bees all buzzed, as if to say,
'No matter what, we'll take your play!'
While butterflies in double dress,
Fluttered by, all in a mess.

Patterns of Silence

In the hush, the crickets chirp,
As frogs in chorus start to burp.
The shadows dance with playful fright,
While owls debate if it's day or night.

Old tree stumps tell their stories grand,
To passing ants, who stop and stand.
In silence, humor weaves its thread,
Through every nook where laughter's fed.

Underneath the Green Tapestry

In leafy halls, the vines do twist,
While caterpillars make a list.
'Wiggle twice, and we'll know why,
The sky is blue, my, oh my!'

The chipmunks in their tiny suits,
Debate on who has the best old boots.
And as the sun begins to set,
They laugh and say, 'We're not done yet!'

The Tapestry of Nature

Leaves giggle as they twirl,
Squirrels plot their acorn dance.
Branches weave a riddle, hurled,
Nature's stage, a wobbly chance.

Birds wear hats made of bright grass,
Bumbling bees in a tuxedo.
Beneath the shade, time does pass,
With shadows playing on the meadow.

A frog croaks out a funny tune,
While butterflies wear silly ties.
Rabbits hop, they start to swoon,
Chasing dreams beneath the skies.

Twirling leaves, a playful tease,
The wind whispers quirky fables.
In this world of leafy ease,
Laughter echoes through the stables.

Echoes Among the Trunks

Woodpeckers knock with a rhythm loud,
While critters hide and peek about.
Silly sounds from a sneaky crowd,
As laughter bubbles without a doubt.

A raccoon spins a tale so grand,
Wearing socks that mismatched shine.
A silly dance, a goofy stand,
Among the trunks, they frolic fine.

In this realm of knotted roots,
Their wacky antics never cease.
Squirrels play silly, furry brutes,
Creating chaos with such ease.

Echoes whisper through the bark,
Cheeky giggles rise like steam.
In every corner, there's a spark,
Of joyful fun, a woodland dream.

Serene Retreat from the Sun

A turtle takes a sunnest snooze,
While shadowy friends play peekaboo.
In cooler spots, they can't refuse,
Beneath a leafy quilt, a sumptuous brew.

Chasing beetles as they glide,
With funny jumps, they take their sport.
In this shade, they twist and slide,
A raucous bash, a revelry sort.

A chameleon mixed, oh what a sight,
Changing colors like a clown.
Sunbathing frogs enjoy the light,
As giggles spread and dance around.

With every rustle, there's a cheer,
In a peaceful yet playful way.
This retreat brings laughter near,
And brightens up a sunny day.

Breath of the Woodlands

In the woodlands where giggles bloom,
Each creature wears its finest flair.
Shenanigans stir up from gloom,
A funny waltz fills the fresh air.

A bear tries to twirl, what a scene,
Stumbling on a fallen log.
While frogs croak out a quirky sheen,
A merry jig through the morning fog.

Ants march in shoes far too big,
Fumbling around in a silly race.
The wind joins in with a little jig,
As nature dons a playful face.

With every rustle, a chuckle flows,
The breath of the woods, a joy untold.
In leaf-strewn paths, where laughter grows,
A tapestry of mirth to behold.

Nature's Quilt Above

Clouds are sheep, fluffy and white,
They bounce around, what a sight!
Trees play hide and seek all day,
Laughing as children run and sway.

The sun peeks out with a cheeky grin,
Tickling the leaves, they giggle and spin.
A squirrel's dance, a wobbly show,
Tripping on branches, oh no, oh no!

Birds in a choir, singing off-key,
Charming us all with their rhapsody.
Nature's laughter fills the air,
A symphony created with utter care.

So next time you're lost in a grove,
Remember the joy and the love to rove.
A quilt of green and a dash of fun,
In playgrounds of whimsy, we all can run!

Swaying in Silence

Leaves are swaying to a funky beat,
Who knew that trees could feel such heat?
A raccoon stumbles, takes a bow,
In the woods, the party's now!

Breezes tease with friendly pokes,
Whispering stories, cracking jokes.
Nature chuckles, oh so sly,
While butterflies just flutter by.

Mushrooms giggle in their hats,
As ants parade with acorn flats.
Caterpillars join with flair,
In dance-offs that go without a care!

So when the trees begin to sway,
Join in the fun, don't delay!
The woodland party's best in light,
Where shadows dance and laughter's bright.

The Foliage's Whisper

Underneath the leafy dome,
Squirrels chatter, making it home.
Trees whisper secrets in the breeze,
Tickling branches, as if to tease.

A chipmunk laughs with a nut in tow,
Filled with bravado, on the go.
Flowers giggle, a colorful sight,
Winking at bees in morning light.

The sun plays tag with shadows long,
While crickets chirp their silly song.
Each rustle partners with a shout,
As nature dances, without doubt!

So step closer, hear the sound,
In the arena of green, joy is found.
The foliage's giggles swirl about,
Join the laughter, there's no doubt!

Nestled in the Greenery

In the hush of green, a whispering prank,
Bushes chuckle by the riverbank.
A frog sings opera with gusto and flair,
While dragonflies jitter, twisting in air.

The flowers argue whose colors are bright,
As bees buzz around in sheer delight.
Grasshoppers leap with a rebellious jump,
Who knew a garden could be such a lump!

Under leaves, a raccoon snores,
Dreaming of snacks, making endless scores.
The wind plays tricks, tickles your nose,
With secrets of mischief that nature knows.

So gather your friends, let laughter flow,
In the greenery's joy, let your spirit grow.
There's fun in each nook, a smile in each turn,
In the wilds of laughter, there's always more to learn!

Embers of Sunlight Below

Squirrels plot aloft, dressed in fur,
Whispering secrets with a playful stir.
They think they're ninjas, oh what a hoot,
Chasing each other in swift-footed pursuit.

Shadows play tag with a breeze so light,
Bouncing off branches, a comical sight.
Sunbeams giggle, tickling the ground,
As laughter of fauns echoes all around.

A rabbit hops in a wild game of haste,
Dodging the dappled, with no time to waste.
Chortles and chuckles fill the bright air,
As nature's wee creatures perform with flair.

In this green realm, the nonsense is king,
Where even the mushrooms have stories to sing.
Each little critter, a performer so sly,
Beneath this vast roof, oh my, oh my!

Embraced by Flora

Flowers dressed in vivid array,
Dance in the wind like a playful ballet.
Bees don tuxedos, buzzing with glee,
At this vibrant gala beneath the great tree.

Leaves giggle softly, their whispers are sweet,
Creating a chorus in nature's heartbeat.
A toad on a lily croaks out a tune,
While butterflies waltz 'neath the warm afternoon.

Fern fronds unfold with a curious grin,
Coaxing the ladybugs to spin, spin, spin!
With every petal that flutters and sways,
Laughter erupts in their colorful plays.

Nature's wild party is never quite still,
The humor of growth is a jubilant thrill.
So come join the bash, it's a merry retreat,
In this leafy embrace, life's joy is complete!

The Forgotten Paths Beneath

Mysteries linger where the shadows yawn,
With whispers of mischief as daylight is drawn.
Tangled vines giggle, they're up to no good,
Planning the antics of the forest's brotherhood.

Old logs tell tales, if only you'd pause,
About raccoons robbing a picnic's cause.
Squirrels can't handle their own cheeky tricks,
As acorns go flying, to nature's quick fixes.

Under the roots where the fairies may dwell,
A gossiping fox spins a mischievous spell.
"Have you heard the one about the lost shoe?"
He chuckles to himself, "It once belonged to a coo!"

Paths winding crooked, with laughter and fun,
In this tangled theater, life's pranks have begun.
Every twist and turn brings a new chance to see,
The whimsy of nature, wild and carefree!

Threads of Light Shining Through

Spotlight beams dance upon leafy floors,
Illuminating giggles from the world it adores.
Laughter from crickets, a night-time delight,
As fireflies twinkle in their glowing flight.

Sun-kissed mushrooms wear polka-dots proud,
While ants march in line, a meticulous crowd.
The queen of the insects, in her tiny abode,
Wonders aloud how this dance has erode.

Clouds peek in, throwing shade with a grin,
"Not my fault," they chuckle, "you're just too thin!"
As shadows swirl, with a playful tease,
Nature's own jesters, dancing with ease.

So come, take a stroll where the rays gleam bright,
In this whimsical world, everything feels right.
With threads of pure joy weaving tales anew,
The forest is chuckling, just waiting for you!

Beneath the Canopy of Stars

At night the squirrels dance and prance,
They trip, they fall, but take a chance.
The moonlight shines on their furry backs,
Who knew these critters loved to relax?

The owls hoot out ridiculous jokes,
While fireflies buzz like glowing croaks.
Twinkling lights in the bushes play,
Is it a party? No, just a buffet!

The raccoons arrive with snacks in hand,
Parenting rules they don't understand.
They giggle and snack on chips and fruit,
Under the stars, they're quite the hoot!

Just be careful not to spill the beans,
Or you might get chased by those furry queens.
In the playful night, there's joy and glee,
When the animals gather for a comedy spree.

Songs of the Forest Floor

The mushrooms chant their silly songs,
As rabbits hop and sing along.
A frog joins in with a loud ribbit,
While the crickets play, oh so inquisit!

Beneath the leaves where shadows creep,
The giggles of the woodland seep.
In puddles, frogs dive, splash, and twirl,
Making ripples like a merry whirl!

A hedgehog spins like a tiny ball,
While ants parade, they're having a ball.
The wind joins in with a cheeky breeze,
Tickling the branches, oh, such a tease!

As dusk sets in, the songs grow loud,
Spreading laughter through the crowd.
In the heart of the forest, life must be,
A concert of absurdity, pure jubilee!

The Hidden Grove

In a grove where trees like giants stand,
A rabbit juggles, it's simply grand!
With acorns flying here and there,
You'd think it's a circus affair!

The chipmunks cheer with tiny bells,
While the tortoise slips and almost fell.
A wise old crow offers advice,
"What's a show without a bit of spice?"

Miss Skunk declares it's time to dance,
With her fancy moves, she gives a chance.
The leaves all shake with the wild beat,
In this hidden world, nothing's discreet!

The sun peeks in for a little flash,
Catching a glimpse of the woodland bash.
With laughter ringing throughout the trees,
Here in the grove, it's sure to please!

Secrets of the Arboreal Realm

Whispers float through the leafy heights,
Of secret tales and woodland delights.
A beaver's joke brings laughter loud,
As the entire forest shares a crowd.

The owls share gossip, how absurd,
About a cat that thinks it's a bird!
With hidden paths that twist and twine,
Each secret's allure is simply divine.

The swings of vines become a stage,
Where every critter acts their age.
A dance-off breaks in the midday sun,
Who knew the tree folk had such fun?

Squirrels hoard not just for the cold,
But for the laughs and stories told.
In this arboreal realm, it's clear,
That fun is the treasure they hold dear!

Mosaic of Light and Shade

Dancing leaves whisper jokes,
Laughter floats on breezy strokes.
Sunbeams peek with cheeky grins,
Tickling toes where mischief spins.

Branches sway like silly hats,
Raccoons prance, the chubby brats.
Squirrels play a game of hide,
While shadows chuckle, side by side.

Worms in soil throw a party,
With earthworms moving all so hearty.
Frogs croak songs of playful glee,
As beetles spin in jubilee.

In this patch of light and dark,
Frolicking sounds, a joyful lark.
Nature's quirks, a comedy,
A treasure trove of hilarity.

Reveries Beneath the Limbs

Beneath the arms of leafy friends,
Where laughter starts, and never ends.
A squirrel quizzes a passing bird,
While mushrooms giggle, quite absurd.

The sun plays peek-a-boo with shade,
And every tree is a grand parade.
Rabbits hop in rainbow socks,
Teasing turtles who wear clocks.

Crickets strike a jazzy beat,
As butterflies dance on nimble feet.
The whole wood laughs with silly cheer,
In this circus, no one's austere.

Here, silly thoughts weave like a vine,
Where every critter is divine.
A tableau of whimsy and delight,
Painting moments in pure sunlight.

When Nature Hides

Nature's funny game of seek,
Where sneaky shadows play hide and peek.
The owl blinks with a sarcastic wink,
While the shy fox studies its drink.

Cool breezes whisper secret tales,
Of bears in hats and silly snails.
A clumsy moose stumbles on a root,
Spinning wildly, giving a hoot!

Ants parade with tiny shoes,
Juggling crumbs as they amuse.
The sky rolls its eyes at the plight,
Of a turtle that forgot its flight.

Here's the world in playful disguise,
Where every critter wears a surprise.
In laughter and antics, we're all entwined,
In nature's comedy, hilariously blind.

The Haven of Sun and Shadow

In the patch where sunshine plays,
And shadows hide in sneaky ways.
A crow cracks jokes about the worm,
Who wriggles back, quite out of term.

The flowers giggle, chasing bees,
While crunching leaves tease the gentle breeze.
Lizards pose on sunlit rocks,
As butterflies mock the tickly socks.

A chattering chipmunk shares a snack,
While toads complain of sunburnt backs.
Rain dances down like laughter bright,
As nature spins its yarns, pure delight!

So come join in, don't miss the spree,
In this haven, wild and free.
Where life's a chuckle, oh what a sight,
In this joyful blend of day and night.

Sunlight Dappled Dreams

A squirrel wore a tiny hat,
While searching for his prize acorn.
He slipped and fell on his own mat,
And laughed as he was still reborn.

The sunbeams danced like silly mice,
With shadows playing peek-a-boo.
A ladybug rolled dice,
To gamble for a partner true.

A butterfly played hide-and-seek,
Among the flowers round and bright.
It tickled with a playful cheek,
Then vanished, giggling into the night.

The breeze whispered secrets sweet,
To trees that swayed in breezy cheer.
They chuckled at the playful feat,
Of nature's joy that draws us near.

Beneath the Verdant Arch

A frog wore shades, a cool allure,
While croaking like a pop star king.
He thought his dance was quite the cure,
For all the pond's most boring things.

Two birds joined in a lively show,
With tweets and chirps in perfect tune.
They'd bust a move, then steal the show,
Beneath the branches of the moon.

A mouse dreamt big of cheese galore,
While juggling nuts he couldn't eat.
He tripped and rolled, fell to the floor,
And laughed at his own tiny feet.

A party here, for all to see,
Nature's laughter, wild and free.

Serenity in Shaded Spaces

With paper hats and picnic snacks,
A penguin tried to mimic owls.
He flapped his wings, forgot some hacks,
And danced around as laughter prowls.

The tortoise hosted a grand race,
While revelers cheered 'til they dropped.
Slow and steady, kept up the pace,
As rabbits snoozed, their dreams well-copped.

A lone snail joined the fun parade,
Resplendent in his slimy shell.
He offered jokes, a slick crusade,
And laughed at how his path would tell.

In this place, where giggles soar,
Fun reigns supreme forevermore.

The Green Embrace

An owl in shades surveyed the scene,
As rabbits danced in funny feet.
A choir of frogs sang off the key,
Their voices harmonized in tweet.

A chameleon played dress-up games,
Changing colors with a flick.
His friends giggled, called him names,
But still enjoyed his color trick.

The trees chimed in with rustling glee,
As butterflies performed a waltz.
A beetle joined, so plucky and free,
Creating art, despite his faults.

In the greenery, smiles abound,
Where laughter's melody is found.

Light Through the Leafy Veil

Sunlight dances on my nose,
A leaf's mischief nobody knows.
It tickles me and makes me sneeze,
While birds above are laughing, geez!

Squirrels plotting mischief near,
With acorns flying, oh my dear.
They scold each other, what a sight,
As I dodge and weave in pure delight.

A branch falls down, a fruit rolls by,
A sudden rush, oh me, oh my!
Nature's joke is played so well,
In this green world, I've found my shell.

So here I sit, with laughter loud,
In leafy spaces, feeling proud.
Must be magic, can't believe,
How nature's tricks are hard to leave!

Shelter in the Boughs

A squirrel waves, calls me to play,
While the wind giggles, what'd it say?
The branches sway, like arms in cheer,
They know the secrets, oh so clear.

I found a gnome, he wears a hat,
He tells me jokes, imagine that!
With mushroom friends, they form a band,
And every tune makes my heart expand.

A breeze brings whispers, curly and light,
Of pranks that happen in the night.
A raccoon's dance that steals the show,
While laughter echoes from below.

So here I stand, beneath these trees,
With silly creatures, all at ease.
Nature's laughter is my favorite sound,
In this carefree world, joy abounds!

Enigma of the Emerald Crown

An owl hoots jokes, both wise and sly,
While shadows play, and breezes sigh.
With branches bowed, a throne of green,
Where leafy kings have laughter seen.

The ants parade, in perfect row,
Marching like soldiers, what a show!
But then they trip, oh what a fall,
With tiny cries, they stall the crawl.

A turtle sings a silly song,
As laughter bubbles all along.
The crowns of leaves, they sway and dance,
In this bright place, who needs a chance?

Among the mysteries, here we find,
Nature's humor, so unconfined.
A world so funny, yet so profound,
In emerald tales, joy is found!

Voices in the Green

The grasses giggle, whisper, puff,
In tangled tales, they never bluff.
A rabbit hops, with big surprise,
As daisies hide beneath their eyes.

The frogs are croaking, bass in tone,
A serenade, yet all alone.
With fireflies winking in the night,
They join the show, a flickering flight.

Gnarled roots grumble, "We're quite wise,
We've seen it all, to no surprise!"
But every time that they insist,
A butterfly flutters, turns the mist.

So let us join this funky spree,
Where laughter lives so wild and free.
In the green realm where humor flows,
Nature's joy, forever grows!

Nature's Hushed Reverie

In the woods, a squirrel's dance,
Chats with birds in a silly prance.
Leaves giggle as the wind does tease,
Nature whispers jokes with ease.

A rabbit laughs at a clumsy hare,
Tripping over roots, without a care.
The trees chuckle, swaying side to side,
As nature's laughter cannot hide.

Frogs wear crowns made of leafy greens,
Host a party where no one's means.
Dance and splash in puddles wide,
While ants prepare their feast inside.

Bumblebees buzz a silly tune,
Swinging high with the flowers in bloom.
In this realm of mirth and play,
Nature's jesters lead the way.

A Haven Among the Giants

Beneath the branches so big and wide,
A hedgehog zips, with a goofy stride.
Tall trees wear hats made of moss,
While squirrels play tag and toss.

A deer with flair prances about,
While a chipmunk thinks it's all a bout.
Frog leaps high, aiming for a snack,
Landing in puddles with a big splat!

A wise old owl, in its raspy tone,
Mocks the crows for their silly moan.
Each creature shares a laugh or cheer,
In this place where no one's drear.

With every rustle and little sound,
Life's a circus, joy abound.
Among the giants, fun is free,
Join the jests, sway with glee!

The Breath of the Canopy

Up in the branches, a monkey swings,
Bragging loudly about its springs.
Leaves hum softly, playing along,
With every note, they sing their song.

Down below, ants march with pride,
Carrying crumbs, a scrumptious ride.
A snail steals glances, slow and sly,
While a flock of birds pass by.

The breeze tells tales of things unseen,
Of mischief managed and moments keen.
Nature's punchlines, quirky and bright,
Chortling in the fading light.

Each whisper of green brings a grin,
For the jests of nature always win.
In this breath of life, we delight,
Laughing with the stars at night.

Under the Arc of Green

Fern fronds bow in a dandy way,
Tickling toes that go astray.
A butterfly prances, all in pink,
Stirring petals with every wink.

Giggling grasshoppers jump about,
Bouncing and chirping, there's no doubt.
Each step is met with flicks and flutters,
Nature's giggles, sweet with utters.

The sun peeks in, making faces bright,
As shadows play, dancing with delight.
In a waltz of laughter and glees,
Joy sways softly among the trees.

With each rustling leaf that cheer,
Comes a chuckle, sincere and clear.
Beneath the greens, laughter whirls,
In the heart of nature, joy unfurls.

Under the Spread of Old Trees

In the shadows, squirrels prance,
Dropping acorns like a dance.
Laughter echoed through the air,
While I dodged the nuts with care.

A raccoon laughed, a joyless sprite,
Stealing snacks, oh what a sight!
Branches creaked with every joke,
As leaves burst forth in fits of smoke.

The wise old owl rolled his eyes,
At foolish antics, more than wise.
Beneath the branches, spirits soared,
Each bird a bard, each leaf adored.

So come and join this wild parade,
Where jesters thrive and pranks are played.
Old trees chuckle at the fun,
As laughter dances in the sun.

A Refuge from the Bright

When beams of sun begin to glare,
We dash for shade, without a care.
A picnic planned, snacks in tow,
But ants had plans; oh, how they glow!

A shady spot became a feast,
The ants rejoiced, and we, the least.
Giggling 'round our crumbly spread,
While bugs planned how to snack instead.

Suddenly, a bird swooped down,
With a goofy flap, it turned around.
It eyed our lunch with beady zeal,
As we all chuckled at our meal.

Bright moments dimmed by silly strife,
In this refuge of munching life.
With chirps and giggles, spirits bright,
We found our laughter, pure delight.

Tales Woven in the Canopy

Amidst the leaves, the stories fly,
Of squirrels plotting how they'll pry.
Branches lean to hear the thrill,
As whispered tales give spirits a fill.

The squirrel said, 'I sighted cheese!'
The birds all shrieked, 'Oh, if you please!'
While beetles laughed, they rolled in glee,
What fun they had on that old tree.

Suddenly, a whisper passed,
Of tales long gone, of dreams amassed.
A wise old crow from high above,
Dropped down some wisdom wrapped in love.

Each laugh, each joke a vibrant thread,
In this woven world, forever spread.
So gather 'round, and take a seat,
For every tale makes life complete.

A Nest in the Teeming Green

In this lush home where life is bold,
The squirrels chatter, their stories told.
A nest of chaos, humor blooms,
As laughter dances in the rooms.

A plump bluebird, once so proud,
Sings off-key to the gathering crowd.
The other birds all rolled their eyes,
"Oh dear, what tunes, it's quite the surprise!"

Below, the critters scurry round,
In search of treasures lost and found.
A laugh erupts, a clumsy fall,
As nature's quirks embrace us all.

So here we dwell in vibrant scenes,
Where joy emerges and life convenes.
Amongst the leaves, the laughter swells,
In our green nest, where humor dwells.

Whispers Beneath the Leaves

Squirrels chattering like old wives,
Trading gossip while the owl sighs.
A raccoon stole my sandwich, it's true,
I wish he'd left the pickle or two.

Flowers doing a silly dance,
Bees join in for a buzzing chance.
A butterfly trip in a flower's lap,
Who knew playing tag could make one nap?

The rabbits have a hoppy debate,
On who can eat the most on their plate.
They judge each other with judging eyes,
While a hedgehog rolls by, full of surprise.

The breeze tickles the leaves with a laugh,
As ants march on in their little path.
They argue about crumbs bigger than them,
But their little world is a gem in the hem.

Shadows of the Timberland

In the shadow, the trees stand tall,
Hosting a party, or maybe a ball.
The owls wear glasses and read the news,
While the foxes sport their party shoes.

Fungi giggle under mushrooms so round,
While the rabbits play leapfrog on the ground.
A bear in pajamas is snoring away,
While a squirrel spins tales of chocolate souffle.

The sun peeks in, a cheeky kid,
With beams of light, playing hide and did.
The shadows stretch like long silly arms,
In the hope of catching the nature's charms.

A hedgehog breaks the silence, oh dear,
By sharing his secret stash of root beer.
The laughter echoes through the leafy maze,
As everyone joins in for a funny craze.

Lullabies of the Forest

Crickets sing soft in a whimsical way,
To soothe the stars that twinkle and sway.
A frog croaks out his melodious vibe,
Making the hedgehogs dance and subscribe.

The mushrooms form a cozy couches,
Where ladybugs host their dance with pouches.
The moon winks at the playful night,
While the fireflies throw a sparkling light.

A sleepy badger counts sheep with glee,
But loses track by counting the trees.
While twilight steals the breath of the day,
The forest giggles before it drifts away.

Sweit dreams dipped in honey tonight,
Will hang on branches until morning light.
And so life hums in a lullaby tune,
As the forest keeps cozy 'neath the moon.

Secrets in the Shade

The turtles gossip, slow but sly,
About the crickets who dance and fly.
A turtle wears a top hat, so chic,
As they gossip and have a hat fashion week!

Vines are twisting like they're line dancing,
While the toads croak with wild romancing.
The shadows play tricks, a slight of sight,
As the fireflies flicker on and off at night.

The shyest deer, with a vibrant flair,
Tries to tell jokes but messes the air.
The trees encourage him, a hearty cheer,
With every attempt the laughter draws near.

In this leafy café, secrets unfold,
With whispers of humor that never grow old.
So let's gather 'round, share stories and play,
For the forest is a jester in its quirky way.

In the Arms of the Woods

Trees have hugging branches, not arms,
Their leafy whispers hide silly charms.
A squirrel laughs at the falling pie,
While shadows dance, waving goodbye.

Bark bites back when I try to lean,
A ticklish tree gives the best green sheen.
Frogs croak jokes by the water's edge,
Even mushrooms wear a playful wedge.

The breeze confesses its ticklish ways,
As I dodge acorns on sunny days.
A woodpecker drums a goofy beat,
While the deer prance on padded feet.

So here I stand, in this earthy show,
With nature's giggles, the best kind of glow.
In the arms of the woods, we all find fun,
Laughing together, until day is done.

Whims of the Wind Through Foliage

Whispers of wind sing through the trees,
Tickling leaves, dancing with ease.
They tease the branches, take them for spins,
While the laughing brook just giggles and grins.

A gust of air plays hide-and-seek,
Chasing after squirrels that play peek-a-boo cheek.
The breeze nudges flowers, making them sway,
As petals flutter in a jazzy display.

The cheeky clouds join in the game,
Rolling around with no sense of shame.
A tumbleweed tumbles with dreadful grace,
Too proud to admit it's a messy race.

So let the wind tell silly tales,
Of frolic and tickles in nature's gales.
With laughter as bright as sun in the sky,
Whims of the wind make the world fly by.

A Canopy of Dreams

A patchwork of leaves weaves up above,
Holding secrets of laughter and love.
Bugs have parties, but invited me late,
They dance with the fireflies, oh what a fate!

Branches bend low, with a curious spy,
Birds gossip loudly as they hop by.
The sun plays peek-a-boo, quite the tease,
While I tell stories to bumblebees.

A chipmunk in slippers prances with glee,
While shadows play tag, hidden by a tree.
The colors of sunset, they shimmer and beam,
In this world where I chase all my dreams.

So come join the fun, let laughter abound,
In this amusing haven where joy can be found.
A canopy filled with puns and more,
Holds every dream on its leafy floor.

The Secret Language of Leaves

Leaves chatter softly in riddles and rhymes,
Cackling like chickens, slipping through climes.
A rustle here, a flutter there,
They share whispers of tales that they dare.

The maple winks with a fantastical tale,
While the oak chortles, quite proud and pale.
A conspiracy hatched by the roots of the trees,
To plot silly games with the buzzing bees.

A leaf took a dive to impress a flower,
While twigs jump around like they've got power.
Their gossip shimmers in the sunlight's glow,
As insects commute, putting on a show.

So listen closely to what they say,
The secret language lights up the day.
Where every rustle can tickle your mind,
In this leafy chat, true silliness you'll find.

Harmony in the Hollow

Squirrels chatter, tails a-twirl,
As acorns bounce and eyebrows curl.
A rabbit hops, thinks it's a race,
While frogs leap by, all over the place.

Laughter echoes in leafy halls,
A raccoon pranks, he's always on calls.
"Catch me if you can!" he yells with glee,
As birds sing songs like a wild jubilee.

Shadows dance like they're on a spree,
With ants forming lines, oh, what a spree!
A sunbeam spills like melted ice,
And every critter rolls with pure delight.

So join the fun in this lush retreat,
Where every path is a joyful beat.
In the hollow, life's a hoot,
With nature's symphony, we all salute!

Murmurs of the Foliage

Whispers flutter, leaves confide,
A beetle laughs; it's quite a ride.
A worm tells tales of garden fame,
While spiders weave their webs of game.

The wind joins in, a playful breeze,
Tickling the branches, bending the trees.
A parrot squawks, "What's the scoop?"
As flowers sway to nature's loop.

In patches of sun, the critters lounge,
While a sleepy sloth grins in his grouch.
The chatter builds from morn to dusk,
In this green realm, there's never a husk.

So come and giggle with every rustle,
For in the greenery, we all must tussle.
With every giggle, the world twirls bright,
In this foliage dance, all feels just right!

Sanctuary of the Silent Trees

Beneath the boughs, the shadows play,
Where bugs and critters lounge all day.
A fox is snoozing, dreams of fish,
While ants parade, making their wish.

A bear in slippers, oh what a sight,
Waltzes through, munching berries bright.
The owls giggle, perched so spry,
With beaks a-twitching, they just can't lie.

Branches creak like old man's knees,
A squirrel cracks jokes, bringing the ease.
The breeze joins in, a tickling tease,
Turning old trees into stand-up peas.

In this haven where silence bursts,
With playful spirits, nobody's cursed.
The trees laugh low as they shield the show,
In this whimsical world, just let it flow!

Chasing Sunbeams

In fields of green, they run and leap,
Chasing sunbeams, not a single peep.
A dog rolls over, paws in the air,
As butterflies giggle without a care.

The clouds are fluffy, a cotton candy,
While kids shout "Catch me!" feeling dandy.
With each jump, they chase the light,
As shadows dance in pure delight.

A cat lounges; it's far too cool,
To join the race—"Time for a snooze!"
While frogs croak songs, singing their part,
As the sun dips low, it warms the heart.

So gather 'round in this golden glow,
Where laughter sparkles and spirits flow.
In the chase of light, life feels so grand,
In this sunny realm, all take a stand!

Shadows Play on Earth Below

Silly squirrels perform their dance,
While sunlight twirls, giving shadows a chance.
Beneath the trees, a picnic feast,
With ants conducting, it's quite the beast!

Laughter echoes from silly folks,
As branches giggle with tree trunk jokes.
With every rustle, a ticklish tease,
Nature's comedy, doing as it please!

The Silent Watchers

Old oaks whisper secrets to the breeze,
While tall pines chuckle, shaking their knees.
A wise old birch gives a sage nod,
As mushrooms giggle from sod to sod.

Who knew a forest could be so sly?
Watch the trees wink as the squirrels fly.
With all this chatter, what can we say?
It's just another hilarious day!

A Symphony of Swaying Branches

Branches sway to a leafy tune,
While birds make music, morning to noon.
A chipmunk tries to sing and croak,
But all he does is make the leaves choke!

The wind joins in with a dancing swirl,
Creating chaos, oh what a whirl!
The forest's concert is quite absurd,
Nature's giggle, the funniest heard!

The Hidden Light

Sunlight peeks through branches tight,
Making shadows that jiggle with delight.
A rabbit hops, thinking it's a game,
Chasing the glow, oh what a claim!

Glowworms laugh, lighting up the night,
As frolicking critters dance in delight.
The moon rolls his eyes, what a sight to see,
In this wild party, nature's jubilee!

Dappled Light and Dreams

A squirrel with a crown, oh what a sight,
He thinks he's a king in the broad daylight.
Chasing his subjects, he leaps with glee,
While birds roll their eyes from the topmost tree.

The sun's playful fingers tickle the floor,
Where ants march in lines, plotting their score.
A picnic of crumbs lays sprawled on the grass,
While butterflies giggle; they just let it pass.

Laughter echoes when clouds drift away,
As shadows dance wildly, they want to play.
A raccoon in the corner steals snacks for a feast,
And the whole forest cheers; "He's a sneaky beast!"

The evening descends; stars wiggle and bend,
While crickets tell tales that just won't end.
A firefly brigade twinkles like a show,
And we all join the fun, saying, "Let's go!"

Beneath the Verdant Arch

A turtle in sneakers, oh what a chase,
He's late for a meeting; he picks up the pace.
Frogs leap in laughter, giving him sass,
As he pants and wheezes, "I'll get there, alas!"

Leaves rustle above with a giggling sound,
When a chubby raccoon scampers around.
"Oh look!" says a crow, "What's he up to now?
Bet he's planning a party, let's take a bow!"

The sun dips low; shadows stretch out wide,
While a family of ducks takes a leisurely ride.
The pond hosts a splash—oh what a delight!
Who knew being silly could feel so right?

Under the branches, the silliness grows,
With jokes that the owls secretly compose.
The night brings a hush; the stars start to wink,
And all the creatures gather for a drink!

Stories Woven in Green

A mouse with a mustache boosts his own fame,
He spins tall tales, each crazier than the same.
A dragon he fought in the bellflower patch,
But truth be told, he was just after a snack!

The trees nod and giggle, swaying in fun,
As the squirrel declares, "Yes, I'm the fast one!"
Each breeze carries whispers, a chorus of joy,
With bugs tapping rhythms like a busy toy.

The plucky little rabbit hops in for a dance,
Tripping over roots but never losing his chance.
"Let's boogie!" he shouts in an enthusiastic hum,
While crickets agree, "We're better with some!"

The evening brings stories from branches so wide,
The laughter erupts, it cannot be denied.
Each character adds to the vibrant din,
Celebrating life in the thick of the spin!

The Embrace of Branches

The breeze rustles softly, like an old friend's tear,
As a raccoon complains, "I'm out of here!"
He fumbles with berries, his nose in a jam,
While the laughter erupts; they go 'Bam-Bam-Bam!'

The picnic ants march, with forks and spoons,
Serving up laughter under the doubting moons.
A rabbit recites his meticulously planned,
"I brought carrot cake; now lend me a hand!"

Owls hoot their approval, taking it slow,
As fireflies dance in a shimmering glow.
"Who's got the best jokes?" the fox bumps a bun,
Let's hear what you got; oh, this will be fun!

Under the branches, where friendships ignite,
The air carries chuckles as day turns to night.
The woodland is buzzing with jokes and delight,
In a place where the laughter takes endless flight!

Veiled in Nature's Embrace

In a cloak of green, the squirrels prance,
While rabbits play their little dance.
A frog gives a leap, and then a stare,
As if to say, 'Do you even care?'

The whispers of trees tell silly tales,
Of giggling winds and perfect fails.
While owls debate who's the wisest one,
The raccoons feast, think they're so fun!

With leaves as hats and twigs as swords,
The critters gather, their own tight hoards.
They laugh and tumble, making a scene,
As though they've formed a woodland queen!

So come take a peek, this joyful show,
Where mischief abounds and giggles flow.
In nature's grand joke, we all participate,
For laughter blooms at a mossy gate.

Dance of the Rustling Leaves

A breeze comes laughing, tickling the trees,
As leaves shake hands with wobbly knees.
They twirl and spin under the bright sun,
While critters cheer, 'This is so fun!'

The chipmunks join in with little hops,
Timing their moves, they never stop.
With acorn hats and twiggy canes,
They boogie down, ignoring their pains.

A hedgehog rolls into the fray,
Confidently saying, 'Let's play all day!'
While a butterfly judges the funky style,
With flutters and flaps that bring a smile.

So let the leaves dance and make a scene,
In this merry forest where all can glean.
Just don't step on a beetle's shoe,
Or the dance-off's done, and we'll all boo!

Guardians of the Woodland

In a huddle of trees, the guardians grinned,
Casting shadows where stories begin.
A funny old bear keeps losing his hat,
Chasing a squirrel—a bit too fat!

The wise old owl wears spectacles tight,
Telling the bugs to keep out of sight.
While rabbits debate who's the fastest around,
With legs like rockets—they leap from the ground!

The porcupine jokes that he's full of spine,
While the raccoon snaps selfies, feeling divine.
With giggles and chatter, they hold their ground,
These woodland friends who are nature-bound.

So if you hear laughter when walking near,
It's the guardians laughing, so give a cheer!
In this leafy haven, where fun's always found,
Nature's the circus, and joy is profound.

The Enchanted Boughs

The boughs of trees bow down for a chat,
With whispers of secrets, like, 'What's up, cat?'
A trickster crow makes a grand ol' mess,
While squirrels in armor play out their quest.

Beneath the leafy stage, a cast convenes,
With chipmunks in capes and acorn machines.
They pratfall and tumble in a grand display,
Making the ants giggle and sway.

The branches chuckle, swaying with glee,
As an owl declares, 'I'm the king of the tree!'
But a gust of wind sends him for a loop,
As all of his subjects dissolve into a whoop.

Amidst this charm, the moments unfold,
With laughter and antics, a tale to be told.
So join in the fun, you poor weary soul,
In this magical realm, let loose and roll!

The Embrace of Boughs

Squirrels practice their stunts,
Rolling like acorns, full of fun.
Each branch a landing pad,
With laughter that can't be shunned.

Birds gossip of the latest trends,
Chirping tales of clumsy friends.
A woodpecker gives a knock,
While a rabbit hops, then bends.

Sunshine peeks through leafy screens,
Where shadows dance in silly scenes.
It's a woodland circus here,
With nature's quirky routines.

In this realm of tangled hair,
Every mishap brings a cheer.
A falling leaf, a clumsy jump,
Turns a solemn day to beer.

Murmurs of the Timber

Old trees tell tales so odd,
A rogue branch sneezes, 'Oh my God!'
With every rustle, there's a laugh,
Twisting humor, nature's prod.

The raccoon wears a leafy hat,
While parading round like he's a cat.
The groundhog shakes its furry fist,
At mischief, claiming, 'I'm a brat!'

Whispers float on gentle winds,
Giggling leaves tell where it begins.
Fallen logs make comfy chairs,
For squirrels discussing silly sins.

Beneath the sky's grand, blue dome,
Every twist connects to home.
Nature's jokes, a riotous spree,
Where the wildlings love to roam.

Glimmers in the Gloom

In shadows where the critters play,
Frogs have disco nights, they say.
Fireflies twirl like tiny stars,
While the owls hoot, 'Let's sway!'

A raccoon steals some picnic treats,
With scruffy paws and quickened feet.
But tripped on roots, it winds up lost,
A tasty snack becomes a feat.

Moss gives way to dancing feet,
As laughter echoes, playful heat.
Each branch a stage, each leaf a cheer,
For forest dreams that feel complete.

At dusk, the shenanigans unfold,
With stories of mischief, proudly told.
Glimmers shine through every nook,
While twigs catch laughs like tales of old.

Beneath the Shelter of Leaves

In cozy nooks, the critters jest,
A turtle claims it knows the best.
Challenging the speedy hare,
To see who's truly blessed.

Rabbits bounce in leaps and bounds,
Jokes are traded all around.
A snail with shades takes a slow stroll,
While laughter in the air resounds.

Wise owls chuckle at the show,
As windblown whispers softly flow.
Heard by creatures of all sorts,
From lively mice to lazy crow.

In this shady haven bright,
Each mishap turns to pure delight.
Life's a giggle in disguise,
Where silliness takes perfect flight.

Veils of Moss and Moonlight

In a world where squirrels take bets,
Who'll win the acorn—take your best!
Frogs croak tunes, their croaks all wrong,
Yet still they dance, all night long.

A rabbit named Tim wears a top hat,
He's famous for juggling with a fat cat.
Owls wear glasses, quite the sight,
Reading stories till the dawn's light.

Toadstools gossip over tea,
"Mushroom soup is all we decree!"
While fireflies play lamps for the show,
A disco ball in the night's glow!

Giggles echo where shadows creep,
And even the trees begin to leap.
With every rustle, a tickle of fun,
In this wild party, there's room for everyone!

Symphony of the Canopy Brush

Beneath the branches, a band plays loud,
Narwhals and crickets attract a crowd.
The raccoons, dressed in tuxedos neat,
Dance on logs with double-tap feet!

A chorus of birds with mics in beaks,
Sing top hits and make their critiques.
One parrot claims it's all too cliché,
"Flip a pancake, it's a brand new play!"

A deer prances while tweeting his friends,
"Who likes this jam? It never ends!"
The trees sway, grooving with glee,
All nature joins, a jubilee spree!

As laughter mingles with rustling leaves,
The night drips magic, no one grieves.
In this weird concert, all things align,
With a wink and a nod, everything's fine!

Whispers of the Leafy Roof

In the shadows where fluff-fluffs play,
A turtle DJ spins night and day.
The bunnies show off their latest hops,
While the fawns plot pranks to make jaws drop!

A snail in shades, oh what a sight!
Struts and slides, he's feeling quite light.
"Who needs speed?" he says with a grin,
"Just take your time to let the fun begin!"

Lizards discuss fashion, which colors to wear,
While squirrels debate—'should we comb or not care?'
The crickets make beats with their legs so swift,
As plants give applause; it's a nature gift!

As giggles bounce off each feathered soul,
This whimsical world has no one goal.
Just moments of mirth in a maze of green,
Crafting joy in this leafy scene!

Shadows Beneath the Branches

In shadows where giggles seem to hide,
Frogs with sunglasses take a ride.
They hop on toads with great delight,
Planning parties that last all night!

A raccoon chef cooks gourmet bliss,
"Who wants the fruit salad? It's hard to miss!"
Berries explode, a blueberry fight,
Sticky and sweet, what a dazzling sight!

The owls roll dice for a game so grand,
While the fawns cheer loudly, a wild fan band.
"Let's win some acorns!" they joyfully scream,
As laughter dances like a wild dream.

So raise your cups made of leaves and bark,
To nights filled with humor that leaves a mark.
In this playful realm, where shadows play nice,
Every moment is gold, what a fun paradise!

www.ingramcontent.com/pod-product-compliance
Lightning Source LLC
Chambersburg PA
CBHW071838160426
43209CB00003B/341